wildly
deserving

A catalogue record for this book is available from the National Library of New Zealand.

Soft cover ISBN 978-0-473-64051-4
POD Soft cover ISBN 978-0-473-65666-9
Kindle ISBN 978-0-473-64053-8
Epub ISBN 978-0-473-64052-1
Apple Books ISBN 978-0-473-64054-5

Cover design by Amanda Sutcliffe

Design & layout www.yourbooks.co.nz

wildly
deserving

LISA BUSCOMB

This book is dedicated to my boys who show me the true magic of the every day moments.

FOR YOU

Words have the power to shape our lives. From the moment you start your day, to your last thoughts as you drift off to dream, the words you think, see, and say have an incredible impact on your daily life - and creating the life you dream of. My empowering words are food for your soul and fuel for your dreams, reminding you to believe in yourself, know your worth, and find the magic in the everyday mundane moments, always. In dark times, these empowering words can be your armour and a daily whisper of possibilities. Every day these words are your inspiration, your friendly reminder, your strength and support.

I wrote this book so you could turn to any page each day, and discover words of inspiration and a reminder that we are all so beautifully unique and yet so similar.

This book is 101 reminders about self-loving, knowing your worth, falling in love with the everyday moments, and trusting that you are wildly deserving.

Lisa x

9-13-23

The real magic of life is when you are
unapologetically you and find the beauty amongst
the *everyday mundane moments.* I write to remind
you that your dreams are yours for a reason. And you
are so *wildly deserving.*

UNAPOLOGETICALLY YOU

I want you to know that you are amazing, even if you feel a little different and a little weird. What if those things about you that you think are flaws, are actually what people love most about you. Are you quiet and introverted? People love that you truly listen and are peaceful to be around. Are you loud & bubbly and excitable? People love that you lift the energy in the room and make everyone smile. Maybe you don't like that you are so emotional, but maybe this is what people love about you, that you are vulnerable. Fall in love with your uniqueness and what makes you unapologetically you. We are all different. You don't need to change. Don't hide the beautiful parts of you. Your unique magic will take you on great adventures & down great paths when you allow it. Let her out. Let her run free and wild and show up in the world. The world can't wait to meet her.

LISA BUSCOMB

This is your daily reminder
that you are amazing,
you are doing an incredible job,
you're beautiful
and are so loved.

HERE'S TO LIFE

Here's to not living from one big life highlight to another. Here's to not feeling like a failure because everything didn't work out perfectly the first time. Here's to not watching others and feeling like you are not worthy. Here's to being unapologetically you. Here's to owning your life, your story, your unique magic. Here's to being the best you that you can be in this moment. Here's to enjoying the slow life, the spaces in between, the quiet seasons of life. Here's to enjoying it all. The whole wild ride. The ups, the downs, the challenges, the wins. Here's to a little trust and a little belief. Here's to knowing in your heart, that you are amazing.

BE YOU

Life tells you that you should do this, or be that. It's so easy to want to make yourself be like those around you. But the truth is things are better when you are you. Things are amazing when you are unapologetically yourself. Life is great when you fall in love with your unique magic. Life is wonderful when you follow your heart, follow what lights your soul and makes your heart happy. Life is good when you follow your dreams. Because you are wildly deserving of all of your desires and you are wildly capable of making your dreams a reality. Simply because, you are you.

I've been thinking that I hope you have the courage to dream big. I hope you have the courage to follow what lights you up and sets your soul alive. I hope you have the courage to share your voice, to stand up for what you believe in, to know that your opinion matters. I hope you have the courage to be more of yourself each day. Because when you have the courage to be unapologetically you, you inspire others to find the courage to be more of themselves too.

DARKNESS

In the darkest seasons, it's the small everyday moments that will guide you through. Those moments that once felt mundane and boring, will now bring peace, stability and happiness. The sunrise starting a new day. The warmth of a hot tea. A soft cosy bed. A delicious meal. Wearing a beautiful outfit. A walk through nature. Watching a long-time favourite movie. A cuddle from a loved one who may not know the whole story but is there for you, in the moment. The magic is in the everyday and when you stop and look around, you realise how amazing this world is. And that even in the dark times, there is lightness.

TIME

Life is a marathon not a sprint. It doesn't matter how fast you go as long as you keep going. There is no such thing as an overnight success. Everyone starts at zero. Those people you look up to? They started at zero. Those people that you are inspired by, they were one day exactly where you are now. They kept going. They took one step at a time, one day at a time. They didn't have all the answers, they couldn't see the final destination but they just kept moving forward. We all need to just keep going. Some days will be hard. Some days will be rewarding. Some days you will literally go round in circles. But every day is part of your journey.

It's time to discover who you are.
It's time to uncover those things that make you
amazing, that make you unique.
It's time to let yourself shine.
It's time to be more you than ever before.
It's time to show up confidently, bravely and
beautifully.
It's time to be unapologetically you.

WELCOME TO MOTHERHOOD

Motherhood. Where love has no limits. Where you wear your heart outside your body every day. Where you try to do the right thing when you're not even sure if it's the right thing. Where the days can be tough but the moments will be magical. Where there's tears, mess, and laughter. Where you lose yourself, then find yourself again, and discover a whole new part of you that you never knew existed. Where you are the comfort that they need. Where one cuddle can change their day around. You are their sun, moon, and stars. You are exactly what they need. You've got this.

I hope you have the courage today to be you.
To be a little more you than yesterday.
And I hope you love this you
because she is pretty damn amazing.

WILD

Life is a wild ride. There are days of perfection and there are days of sheer despair. But every day is a part of your journey, every day brings you closer to where you need to be. Every day will bring you something. Find the little things in the everyday. If a day doesn't go to plan, don't throw it all in, don't give up. Take a breath. Tomorrow is a new day. A chance to start fresh. Wake up with the wonder of what the day could bring you. It's a wild ride this life.

It's time to exhale.
It's time to release.
It's time to just let it be.
It's time to pause.
And then take a step forward.
A small step. Any step.
Even if you don't know where you are going.
Especially if you don't know where you are going.
When you can't see the path ahead,
just take one step.

TO KNOW

At the end of the day, it is important to know that you are not perfect, and that is okay. To know that you are not for everyone, but you are for someone. To know that you are beautifully unique. Heal the parts of you that need healing. Ask for support. Rest and spend time alone. Uncover those beliefs holding you back. Rewrite those thoughts that are stopping you from reaching your greatness. Because the truth is, the more you know you are beautifully unique, the more magic life becomes.

As the stars shine bright in the night sky
Look up and trust
That you already know.

I am limitless
I am deserving
I am abundant
I am worthy
I am enough
I am beautiful
in my own unique way.

POSSIBILITIES

What if everything you are dreaming of is coming to you. What if something even better is on its way. We can get so focussed on what we think we want that we forget to be open to more. We don't see all the possibilities, opportunities, and magic that surrounds us. The people we have just met that have come into our life for a reason, or that thing that is falling away but we are holding on tight. Let it go. When we let things go, we create more space for something new. What if everything you are dreaming of is coming to you, just not in the way you are imagining it.

Give yourself permission
to live a *creative* life.

MINDSET IS EVERYTHING

You are on your own journey where everything is possible. Believe in yourself. Trust in yourself. You know that you can achieve it. You know that your dream can be your reality. Create your life the way you want to. Don't let someone else's idea of success be yours. You choose your own adventure. You have time. Go at your own pace. There is space for you. People want what you are creating. Allow them to discover you. It can be scary but you are courageous. It only takes a moment of courage. And that one tiny step forward could turn into a giant leap. I know you've got this. I believe in you. Do you believe in yourself?

TODAYS SELF-CARE

living in the moment
but with a clear vision for my future.
drinking water
moving my body
early night & restful sleep.
creating the moments I dream of
knowing that it is all on its way.
being unapologetically me
every day.
being grateful for all that I have.
surrounding myself with amazing women
and always remembering
to love on myself.

YOU CAN

You can do it. Even though sometimes you doubt
yourself. Sometimes you feel overwhelmed.
Sometimes you feel like it's too much. Try not to worry.
What good does worrying do? Stop. Take a breath. Or
ten. Dance, laugh, go outside, or call a friend. And then
come back to yourself. Make a plan. Ask for help. Trust
yourself. You are capable of amazing things. And I just
know you are creating the life you dream of. Even if
you can't see it yet.

THIS MOMENT

You are doing the best you can right in this moment. It may look messy, it may feel out of control, it may be nothing like you imagined. But you are doing the best you can. You are showing up, you are taking small steps, you are moving forward. You are doing the best you can with what you've got. Give yourself permission to breathe, to accept this moment. Give yourself time to sit in the messiness. You may be just waiting to get to the other side, but know this moment is here to help you grow. There are lessons to be had, there are moments to be treasured. And know you will get there. This is only a fleeting moment. Although it may not feel like it, you are doing the best you can with what you have right in this moment.

Daydreams are good for the soul.

PLANS

You don't always need a plan. So often society tells us we must have goals, a 5 year plan, a 10 year plan, a to-do list, an action list. But sometimes it's okay just to dream. To daydream about all the possibilities and opportunities without knowing which path you will take. Sometimes it's okay to just wander, to just be. Sometimes it's okay to just breathe, to sit in the unknown. Because often the most beautiful ideas, the best inspiration comes from the quiet. From the daydream. From the space that isn't filled with a plan or a goal.

I am brave
I am strong
I am beautiful
I am confident
I am loved
I am enough
I am me.

TODAY

It's okay if today didn't go as you hoped it would. If you didn't get those projects finished or tick off all on your to-do list. Some days are just for being. For breathing, for gazing out the window, for being in the moment. Every day doesn't have to be productive. Tonight, you can go to sleep knowing that you did the best you could in the moment. And tomorrow is a new day.

REGRETS

Never regret. Every experience in your life has bought you to this moment. And this moment is perfect. Your childhood, your early years. All the years as you grow are part of your who you are today. It is never a waste of time. There is nothing to regret. There are highlights and struggles. There are proud moments and sad moments. Every moment has brought you valuable lessons and new learnings. Learnings about yourself, about your life, about what makes you uniquely you. And those dark moments, the moments with the deepest pains, those are the moments that you really find yourself and your true potential. It is never a waste of time.

She is wild and free.
She is and is becoming.
With every new day she grows and evolves.
In the sunshine and in the storms.
It's all part of her. It's all part of you.
You are wild. You are free.
You are unapologetically you.
Honour yourself and step into your light.

THINGS TO DO MORE OF

fall in love with the small things
know that success looks different for everyone
light that candle on the shelf
use the fine china
allow your heart to open
eat foods you love
deep belly laughs
make time for yourself
watch the sunrise and sunset
trust in the magic
be unapologetically you.

THIS ROAD

The road you are about to travel is not one you dreamed of, or probably ever thought you would find yourself on. But this new journey will be everything you need. You will learn things about yourself you never knew were part of you. You will find bravery, strength, kindness, and love. You will discover magic within you and you will unearth your true self. This is a new journey, a new beginning and even though it's scary, just know this new road is meant for you.

YOU ARE NOT FOR EVERYONE

People are who they are. And whether you agree
with all that they are, is not your responsibility, or your
business. Accept others as they come. They may be
a beautiful addition to your life or they may not be for
you at all. If they are not for you, release them. Let
them go and move on. You are not for everyone, and
everyone is not for you.

LIGHT FOLLOWS DARKNESS

This is your daily reminder that light always follows dark, there are no rainbows without rain. Life is made up of beginnings and endings, highs and lows; flowers don't bloom all year and the sun isn't always shining. If you are currently in a space of darkness, know that the light is on its way.

UNEXPECTED

Life can be unexpected. But sometimes you need unexpected moments. As it's these moments that take you to places you never dreamed of, but in the end, are so perfect. Because it can be so easy to live in your own space; close to home; cosy, safe. The comfort zone. But sometimes it's not until you step outside the comfort zone that you realise what has been waiting on the other side for you. You have been so immersed in what's right in front, that you missed something magical right beside you. And that is why unexpected moments happen, to bring you closer to what is meant for you. To show you new possibilities and potential. To allow your life to fall into place. To create beauty and magic.

ENJOY THE LITTLE THINGS

Rise early and watch the sunrise.
Sit in stillness and breathe.
Read 10 pages of that book.
Chat deeply to a friend.
Enjoy a walk in nature.
Start that creative project on your mind.
Put your feet up and watch the sunset.
Cook a delicious nutritious meal.
Relax in a deep, warm bubble bath.
Early to bed, slow meditation, restful sleep.

THE HARDEST DAYS

And even on the hardest days when you are completely doubting yourself, know there are others in awe of your magic. They are inspired by what you create, by your inner beauty and your unique essence. They can see how truly amazing you are. Just for a moment, can you see what they see?

WORRYING

You have to stop worrying about them. What they think isn't what matters. What they think isn't going to make your dreams come true. In fact, listening to what they think is holding you back. Listening to them is blurring the truth as to who you really are. Stop hiding and pretending you are someone that doesn't matter. You matter. Start sharing your magic. Start sharing who you really are. Start being you. Be confident in what makes you unique. They can't see all of you. They can't see all the dreams, beauty, and magic inside of you. Their opinions don't matter. Your opinion matters. You matter.

KINDNESS

There is not enough kindness in the world. Kindness is not about agreeing with all people, all ideas and all opinions. Kindness is respect, listening, and allowing. Kindness is giving someone space to be themselves, wholeheartedly their unique self. We never know what lies behind closed doors, the pains, and struggles that others are feeling. So share a smile, a hello, or a listening ear. A small gesture can mean so much in a time of struggle. Simply listening could change someone's day around. It's the little things, small acts of kindness that may not seem a big gesture but could mean the world to someone else. You don't always need a reason to be kind. How could you spread a little kindness today?

SLEEP

And at the end of the day, you can sleep well knowing you are worthy. Knowing that you are beautiful inside and out. That you've done the best you can with what you have. That someone is in love with you right now. That you are so incredibly deserving, valuable and treasured. You can sleep well knowing you are amazing and so loved.

NOW

Take a moment for yourself today. Breathe deep. Sit in stillness. Light the candle. Watch the flame. And dream. Daydreams are good. Fall in love with where you are right now. It may not seem perfect, but it is. Enjoy the now. Your dreams will come. Enjoy the small joys, the little things. Breathe deep. Have compassion for yourself. Remember how far you have come.

FALLING

Fall in love with yourself. Fall in love with taking care of you. Fall in love with taking care of your skin and your body. Wash your makeup off before you sleep. Drink water. Wear sunscreen. Eat nutritious foods. Smile. Laugh. Look loved ones in the eye. Look at yourself in the mirror. Really look at yourself in the mirror. And smile. Fall in love with yourself. Gently, with heart, with compassion, with patience. You are worthy of loving yourself. You are worthy of being loved.

THIS TIME

It's okay if everything doesn't work out the first time. Even if you put your everything into it and it doesn't work out the way you dreamed it would, you still won. You showed courage, you showed bravery, you showed determination. You showed that even though you were scared, you still took that step. And while it may not have worked out this time, you have grown, you have learned and you have shown a strength that will take you far.

STRENGTH

You are stronger than you believe. You can do hard things. Through all the tears, fears, frustrations and pain; you will get to the other side. You will learn and you will grow. It may not seem like it right now, but you can do this. I believe in you. When you're struggling, dig a little deeper. You have this in you. And when you get through this you won't be the same person you are in this moment. You will be different but you will still be you, a new version of you. And one day you will look back and be proud of the road you travelled.

YOU CAN GO SLOW

Start a conversation with someone new
Write down the details of your dream life
Take a long hot shower
Enjoy a deep massage & release
Feel good about asking for support
Be spontaneous & do something unexpected
Eat the foods you crave
Know that life isn't perfect
Take in a new view
Discover fresh ideas, inspiration & thoughts.

DREAMS

I can see the sparkle in your eye and the dream in your heart. I see you making progress, working in the nights and early mornings to make those dreams happen. You are working silently, transforming, growing, creating and evolving. You are making progress. It may seem small but every step is a step in the right direction. And one day you will pause and look back, and be in awe of what you have created.

RUSHING

Sometimes we really want to rush through life. Tick the boxes, achieve the goals, turn dreams into reality and create the evidence that proves we are worthy. But what if we can believe we are doing great things without the need to rush. Without all the endless achievements. What if we can see our greatness in the slow times, in the quieter seasons. What if the seasons where we relax a little and trust that everything will work out just fine, become the most memorable. Life is a ride and it's not always the destination that leaves the biggest imprint on our hearts. The road we travel is where all of the magic lies.

And there you were thinking that wishes never come
true. But right in the moment, right in front of you,
is something that you always dreamed of. If only
we gave ourselves the time to look back at how far
we've come once in a while.

PASSION

Do you know how many people dream of finding their passion? Of finding something that they love, that lights them up. Do you know there are so many people who look at you in awe because you are following that dream? You can't give up. You can't not give it your all. You can't not take it as far as it needs to go. Keep following your heart. Keep following your dreams. Keep creating and doing and being. It doesn't matter how fast you go. Slow and steady is perfect. Don't give up. Your passion is yours for a reason.

FALL BACK IN LOVE WITH YOURSELF

Wake early & stretch
Look in the mirror & truly smile
Breathe and sit in silence
Write down all that you are proud of
Paint your nails with your favourite colour
Buy yourself your favourite flowers
Wear that beautiful dress
Enjoy a luxe cocktail with a friend
Curl up in front of a fire with a good book
Tell someone you love them
Thank yourself for all that you are.

SUMMER SUNDAYS

Here's to golden sunrises, sleep ins and slow chats. Here's to breakfast in the sun with your feet up. Windows open, breeze blowing, hair down, bare feet on the ground. Here's to the smile of someone you love, giggles and joy. Here's to soaking in the small things. Here's to walks in the sand, the sounds of nature and clear blue skies. Here's to being in this moment. Discovering the happiness that is always right in front of you. I hope you never grow tired of the beauty of a summer Sunday.

SLOW

It's okay to grow slow. Slow and steady growth still has beautiful magic to it. Maybe in this moment you are not growing forward but you are growing deeper. You are learning, evolving, and becoming. The lessons you are learning are all part of your growth. And maybe these lessons are what is needed most. Every tiny step is moving you forward, and moving you closer. Find peace in the moments in between. Find love for the quiet spaces and the slow growth. Fall in love with where you are going, not how long it takes you to get there.

IT'S OKAY TO

Change your mind
Feel not at your best
Change your dream
Ask for support
Cancel plans
Feel scared
Not know what's next
Say no
Create boundaries
Feel nervous.

SMALL THINGS

As I grow, I'm discovering that I am drawn more to the slow life. To the small things. I look for more simplicity, more meaning, and more slow moments. It's the small things that I'm finding are the true essence of life. They often seem insignificant at the time but they bring real happiness. Warm hugs with loved ones, hot tea, a walk in the sunshine, and a day at the beach. Doing more of the small things makes life truly beautiful. Reading a page-turning book, eating a cookie, drinking champagne, calling a friend, writing a letter, or lighting a candle. Please take this as a little reminder to do something every day that may seem little but makes you smile. Because when you smile, so much feels amazing.

HAPPINESS

And one day you discovered that you can choose happiness. You can choose joy. You can choose to smile. Because even if everything isn't perfect, when you focus on the little things, the small joys, there is always a space to find happiness. The loving cuddles, the hot shower, the 'I love you' text, the delicious meal. There are always beautiful moments in the everyday. And every day you can choose happiness.

CHOOSE YOU

Choose you. Choose you every day. Choose your dreams, your happiness, what makes you feel good. It's okay if you are single, don't have a million-dollar business, haven't yet bought your own home. Maybe these things aren't right for you, yet. Society puts so much pressure on its own ideals. But what are your ideals? You can be different. You can choose you. Choose what lights you up and sets you free. Even if it looks different from what others do. Especially when it looks different to others. I know you feel the pressure but being in alignment with who you truly are, is the most beautiful place to be. You do you. Find the courage and strength to step into being you and watch the magic unfold.

Today, I hope you remember that you are worthy,
you matter and you are so loved; not because of all
that you do but simply because of who you are.

WATCHING

I see you, watching her, worrying that's she's doing so well and is so successful. I see you wondering why you aren't as successful. But let me share this with you. You are already successful. You are exactly where you need to be. It may not be where you dream to be but right now it's perfect. Don't be so hard on yourself. You are worthy. Your dreams are coming together, everything is working out.

PURPOSE

There is a little voice inside your head or a feeling in that space in your gut that tells you this is the right dream for you. There is a little something there, a little knowing that keeps tapping on your shoulder. But it also doesn't make sense. Those around you tell you you're crazy, it will never work. But what if you are right and they are wrong. But it's not even about being right or wrong, it's all about living life in full. It's about following the crazy dreams, the big ideas, the excitement, the nudge, even when they are little. Life is about following what lights you up. And really, what if you are right, what if this little thought is going to bring you everything you ever dreamed of. Trust in you.

ONE DAY

One day you will wake up and that thing you always dreamed of will be here. It will be right in front of your eyes. You will be able to touch it, see it, feel it, know it. You will pause and be amazed at what you have created. You will be proud of what you created. You will feel the excitement and you will feel the exhale. The biggest exhale. Because you finally did it. You actually did it. You created the vision, worked on your dream, and you bought it to life. Congratulations beauty, you deserve it.

Fall in love with yourself
Know that whatever you do today is enough
You are so worthy
Of love
Of happiness
Of dreams
Of being you
Fall in love with your unique magic
Know that you are enough.

FOLLOWING

If you have discovered your passion, what lights you up, what brings you joy; please follow it. Please follow that dream, that desire, that little something in you that you can't stop thinking about. So many struggle to find their passion. So many don't know their greatest desires. You are one of the lucky ones. You are one of the ones that knows what makes your heart swell and your spirit shine. Don't give up, don't push it aside, don't ignore it. It will chase you anyway because it is yours for a reason. Keep going, keep believing, keep taking small steps. It doesn't matter how fast you go, all that matters is that you follow your passion and believe in yourself.

YOUR STORY

You are the author of your own story. And your story matters. Sometimes the book isn't written in the way we imagined when we first sat down to write. But let's embrace the plot twists, the forks in the road, and the sliding doors moments. Let's embrace it all not turning out how we hoped. Let's embrace our unique story. Life is full of chapters, some are breath-taking while others are heart-breaking. But every chapter creates our unique story. Every chapter can be created with love. Every chapter we will look back on and we will discover that everything has a way of working out. Sometimes even better than we imagined. You are the hero of your story. You are an inspiration to many. You matter. Your story matters.

RAW MOTHERHOOD

There is a real juggle to motherhood. A juggle between your children seeing the real, raw, authentic you, and seeing the picture-perfect mum. I know you want your children to see you as the safe space and the strong one. But maybe we teach them more when you let them see the real unique you. Let your children see you following your dreams, setting goals, working towards them, believing in them; and doing what you love. Let your children see you rest, take a break, focus on self-care, and love on yourself. Let your children see you fail or not make the goal. Let them see how it makes you feel and how you move on, what you do next. Let your children see all the emotions, because they are feeling them too. And when you share, you make it all less scary. That is when you create the safe space. There is so much beauty in authenticity, vulnerability, and being real.

TRUST

It is time to trust yourself. It is time to believe in yourself. no matter what has happened before, now is the time to know that you get to create the life you dream of. You get to dream it, to believe it, to take inspired action, and to watch it become your reality. It is time to believe in the magic, to have the knowing that everything is going to work out. Yes, the past has been hard. You've made mistakes, you've wished things were different, you've worried that you aren't enough. But you are enough. You are worthy. You are amazing. You can and will do incredible things. When you trust yourself. When you believe in yourself. It's time. You've got this.

I followed my heart
and *everything* changed.

HOPE

I hope you don't live a life constrained by shoulds. I hope you don't live a life constrained by society's expectations. I hope you don't live a life doing what you think you should do. I hope your life is free. I hope your life lights your soul and warms your heart. I hope your life is a space where your dreams become your reality. I hope your life is big, beautiful, memorable, and unconstrained. I hope your life is exactly what your heart desires. I hope you follow your heart today and every day.

IT'S OKAY NOT TO BE OKAY

It's okay to not be okay. It's okay to feel like tomorrow isn't coming fast enough. It's okay to reach out for help. It's okay to say that you are not okay. Nothing blooms all year. Life is made up of seasons. Seasons of the best times, seasons that just pass by and seasons full of challenges. If you're struggling, know that tomorrow is another day. Know that this too shall pass. Know that you are loved.

DREAMS

The dreams you have in your heart are there for a reason. They are yours because you have the unique magic to bring them to life. Trust it. You may feel afraid, you may feel not worthy, you may feel that your dreams are insurmountable. But you have everything you need within you to bring them into reality. Maybe you will try to ignore them, maybe walk away, maybe push them aside and say no. But they'll keep coming back. Your dreams don't leave you. They are your purpose, your deepest desire. They stay in your mind, in your heart, in your soul. They are always there. And this is your reminder to take a step towards them. Take one small step, just one action that will take you closer. And then take the next small step. And the more you trust and the more you believe, the more you will see. And when the dream is in front of your eyes, you will smile. And you will wonder why you ever doubted yourself.

Read the book
Have the conversation
Make the decision
Speak the truth
Move your body
Treat yourself
Drink more water
Laugh
Trust
Love.

THE MIDDLE

Are you in the messy middle? That time in between taking those first steps of your magical dream, and reaching the moment when your desire becomes your reality. The most challenging time is in those middle moments. It's mundane, it's a slog, it's boring, it's hard and it's not a lot of fun. But it's necessary, it's important. And it's in the messy middle, those spaces in between, where you build your resilience, your patience, and really get to know yourself. And with trust and tenacity, whilst celebrating the small wins, you keep going, even when it feels hard, and you will reach the end. You will receive your magical dream. And you will look back with joy at how far you came. Of how you grew, evolved, and became someone to be so proud of.

Go where your dreams take you.
Take that small step.
Take the step even when you don't know where it will take you.
Especially then.
You don't need to know the whole path.
You only need one right action.
Trust yourself.
What are you feeling.
What do you think you could do next.
Do that.
Trust, believe, you've got this.

A MOTHER'S REMINDER

To be the best mother to your children, you need to be the best you that you can be. It's time to make yourself a priority, take care of yourself, and create the life you dream of. Focusing on you first and filling your cup allows you to be in a space of healthy mind, healthy body & healthy soul. This will allow you to make clear decisions, stay authentically true to who you are, and love yourself. The happiness & joy that you fill yourself up with will naturally pass down to your children, and through to the relationships around you. Fill your cup first and watch the magic.

chase that *dream*.

ONE STEP

Don't say you'll do it one day. Get started today. Take one small step. Do just one thing that will move you closer to your dream. You don't have to know the full path ahead; you only have to take one step in the right direction. The more steps you take, the more the path ahead will illuminate. The more you trust in your dream, the more it will become your reality. It will start surprising you, the things that are happening. Maybe you will think they are coincidences, but they were always meant to be. It's time to start creating your dream. Don't focus on the fear, focus on the opportunities. Every journey has begun with one step. Take one small step.

TODAY

If you are struggling or in a dark place, please know that your dream life is not far from where you are now. Write down what your dream life looks like. Write down what you want, how you want to feel, what you see in your dreams when you close your eyes. Write it all down. The details, the feelings, and visions. Then start visualising this dream as already your reality. Add today's date to the top of the page. This is the date that you start your new journey. The date you start to love yourself again. The date that you start being unapologetically you and owning your beautiful unique magic. It may feel scary and daunting, but you are courageous, you are brave, you can do this. It can be easy to let time pass by. It can be easy to believe things will change or will get better on their own. And maybe they will. But when you decide, that today is the day, how beautiful will it be when you look back on this date and know that this is the day it all began.

RIGHT TIMING

You don't have to have it all figured out. Your job, your career, your relationship, your hopes, and your dreams. It is okay to just be. It is okay to not know and yet still be happy. The answers will come. The answers will come as you live your life. As you take on new adventures, say hello to new people, say yes even when you feel scared. When you honour yourself and your unique magic. When you are truly you, the answers will come. Own your space, own your presence, be the main character of your life. And it will all work itself out, perfectly, at exactly the right time.

TO BE A MOTHER

Here's to being a mother and a sensual, beautiful woman. Here's to loving on others and loving on yourself. Here's to being in the mundane and having big dreams. Here's to being a partner and being unapologetically you. Here's to feeling exhausted and feeling inspired by life. Here's to knowing this too shall pass. Here's to living in the moment, the messiness, the busyness, the loud moments, and the quiet moments. Here's to knowing that this time, whilst a crazy wild journey, will be one forever etched in your memory.

I AM ME

I am brave, strong, one-of-a-kind, powerful, creative, fearless, kind, grateful, enough, happy, evolving everyday, magical, making my dreams a reality, confident, beautiful, deserving of good things, radiant, strong, successful, important, positive, myself, worthy of all I desire, self-aware, supported, joyful, resilient, healthy, peaceful, soft, grounded, fun, adventurous, playful, curious, unique, amazing, and loved. I am creating the life I dream of. I am me.

A JOURNEY

I know you don't feel like you have made it yet. That you aren't where you want to be. But I want to remind you that where you are right now is perfect. Everything is falling into place and happening in a perfect way. It may not feel like it, but trust, it's all going to be okay. Exhale, breathe, relax your shoulders. The road you have travelled to here has not been easy, but life isn't a straight simple smooth path. Life is rocky, and bumpy. But where you have been has brought you here. And the same road will take you exactly where you want to go, or somewhere even better than you could ever imagine. So trust, breathe out, know that everything is falling into place and happening in the most perfect way.

SIMPLE THINGS

Life is living in the moment. In this moment. Enjoying the small things. Now is what matters. Now is where the pure happiness can be felt. Not yesterday, not in the future. When you focus on this moment, you discover the simple things. And the simple things create the memories. At the end of this life you won't be thinking about if you had the biggest house or best job. You won't be thinking about how many Instagram followers you had or if your video went viral. You will be thinking about the family dinners, the sunrises and butterfly kisses. You will be thinking of the quiet conversations, long snuggles and laughing with loved ones. You will be thinking of the simple things. Because in the end that is all that matters.

A BEAUTIFUL LIFE

I've been thinking, that life isn't really about all that you achieve or that your dream comes true exactly as you hoped it would. A beautiful life is about the journey and adventures along the way. A beautiful life is when you kept going even when things felt hard. A beautiful life is experiencing the new paths that you weren't expecting. A beautiful life is the people you meet along the way. A beautiful life is simply, life. All of it. It's not the end, it's not the achievement, it's not the destination. It's every day and every moment along the way.

DUALITIES

At the end of the day it is okay to be brave and scared at the same time. To love traditions and also be inspired by future thinking. To thrive on routine and also enjoy the excitement of spontaneity. It's okay to be realistic while also a risk-taker and a game-changer. It's okay to be strong and simultaneously vulnerable. Life is made up of dualities and you never have to choose only one path. It's okay to be a beautiful blend of two sides, even in the same moment.

A LITTLE ADVICE

If I could give you one piece of advice, it would be this. Define what success means to you. Success isn't always a million dollars in the bank, a 7-figure business, having a fancy car, overseas holidays, and trendy labels. Success is waking up every day smiling. Success can be a home filled with loved ones. Going to sleep each night happy. Knowing that you are following your dreams. Doing more of what lights you up. Success is not the same for you or me. Success doesn't lie within society's ideals, success lies within you. And the biggest mistake you can make is following someone else's idea of success and leaving your dreams behind.

PERFECT

I hope you realise how everything in your life has brought you to this moment. It has all brought you here. All of those challenging moments where you discovered courage and resilience. All of those wonderful moments filled with such joy and happiness. All of those mundane days that sometimes felt like they would never end. I hope you realise that every moment has brought you to today. And where you are today and who you are today is okay. It is perfectly okay.

You would be surprised who is watching your journey, is feeling inspired by it, and is right there behind you supporting you the whole way.

BELIEVING

It is time to trust yourself. It is time to believe in yourself. no matter what has happened before, now is the time to know that you get to create the life you dream of. You get to dream it, to believe it, to take inspired action, and to watch it become your reality. It is time to believe in the magic, to have the knowing that everything is going to work out. Yes, the past has been hard. You've made mistakes, you've wished things were different, you've worried that you aren't enough. But you are enough. You are worthy. You are amazing. You can and will do incredible things. When you trust yourself. When you believe in yourself. It's time.

FALL

Just as the summer fades, the autumn winds arrive and change is in the air. Embrace the change. Because without change you are simply standing still. And standing still holds no inspiration, no motivation, no fun, or no space. Embrace the change of the seasons. The world around us is always changing, always evolving, always moving. Embrace the Autumn feels. Slowing down. Warm drinks. Warm socks. Long cuddles. Enjoy the view because before long it will be changing again.

THINKING

I've been thinking about all the things I have. All the things I am grateful for. All the things that are going right. I've been thinking about the small things, and the big things too. The cool mornings with a hot coffee. Snuggles from loved ones. Time to walk in nature. Space to rest and breath. I've been thinking about all the things I have. The nutritious meals. The warm shower and a soft bed. Friends who call to check in on me and family who love me. I've been thinking about all the things I have and not the things I don't. And everything changed, just while I was thinking.

MOTHERHOOD

Motherhood can be hard. But it's also beautiful and magical. It's so many things intertwined. A challenge and a blessing. A struggle and a joy. It lasts a lifetime and passes by in moments. Don't forget to take time out for yourself. You look after others best when you are looked after. Take care of you. Give yourself love, space and kindness. You are doing amazing. Your children look up to you like you are the one special star shining the brightest in the night sky. And that is absolutely who you are.

There is something so beautiful
when you finally say yes to yourself.
when you take that first step
when you believe that you can
even though you are scared
even when you don't know where it will lead,
especially then.

HOME

When things feel like they're falling apart around you, come back home. To your physical home, to your loved ones, to yourself. Make your home a beautiful place to be. Tidy, light a candle, pick flowers from the garden, open the windows and let fresh air in. Love on your family. Hug, laugh, play, rest, watch a movie, play a board game, spend time together. Take care of yourself. Eat nourishing foods, drink more water, take a walk in nature, sit in stillness. When things feel like they're falling apart around you, come back home.

9/28/23

HARD

It's okay if today was hard. It's okay if nothing went to plan. If it wasn't your best day, if it wasn't a great day, or even a good day. It's okay if it was pretty damn terrible. It's okay if you spent all day waiting for the day to end. We all have those days. Every single person on this earth has bad days. It's life. We all have moments of struggle. But we keep moving forward. Today was one small day in your big full life. And tomorrow is a new day. A day to start fresh. A day to try again.

WAITING

It is okay to be in this space. The transition, the messy middle, the space in between. You've moved on but you haven't yet arrived. You've left behind what you needed to, but the puzzle pieces haven't all yet come together. There is messiness. There is waiting. There is uncertainty. You are wanting to rush but everything is moving slow. You are wondering if you will get to where you want to go. But where you are is perfect. The messy middle is for doors to close and new doors to open. This transition period is where things come undone so that they can be put back together. This is a season of just being, of trusting. This is a season to pause and take a breath. Have love for yourself, you are exactly where you need to be.

Be your biggest cheerleader. Celebrate the small wins. Rest when you're tired. Count your blessings. Learn something new. Take time away from technology. Cry if you want to. Talk to a friend. Hug your kids. And never forget to celebrate your wins - big and small.

I hope you know that
You are amazing
You are wonderfully unique
You have come so far.
You may not be where you want to be yet
But you will get there.
You have to trust.
You have what it takes.
Everything you need is within you.
You are so wildly deserving of your dreams.

FALL IN LOVE WITH THE EVERYDAY MOMENTS

summer days
warm nights
resting & pausing
spending time with yourself
being in nature
swimming in the cool water
nourishing food
loving on your family
early nights & slow mornings
watching the sunrise
new beginnings.

THE EVERYDAY MOMENTS

A life well-lived is when you fall in love with the mundane everyday moments. You may think they are boring, but the truth is, those everyday simple moments create the true magic. Fall in love with enjoying a hot coffee in a beautiful mug, and doing nothing else at the same time. Fall in love with watching the sunrise in silence. Fall in love with making your bed so it is beautifully ready for you at the end of the day. Fall in love with a long hot shower, your favourite scented soap, and a luxuriously soft towel. Fall in love with lighting the candle and enjoying the fragrance. Fall in love with a slow-cooked meal, a movie night on the couch, and snuggling your loved ones. Fall in love with the little things, the small things, the mundane everyday moments. Because those moments. They are the ones that create a beautiful life.

You have a fire in your soul
and courage throughout.
You have passion in your eyes
and love in your heart.
Chase that dream.
Live that beautiful life.
It's all yours for the taking.

RUSHING

You rush, you race, you move fast. You are always looking for the next thing. The next challenge, the next accomplishment. But what if you just paused. If you just took a breath. If you took a moment. If instead of looking into the future, you looked at what is right in front. What if you stood still and looked around. Because what you may find is that now looks perfect. What you will discover is that now is exactly where you need to be. Because if you are always looking to the future, you will miss the magic of now.

WORTHY

And some days you don't feel worthy, or beautiful, or special. But on those days, when you get up, take a deep breath in, pause, exhale and keep going; you show yourself how truly worthy, beautiful and special you are. Because it's your trust and love for yourself that really matters.

MAGIC

The magic isn't in the big moments, the big events, the big achievements. The true magic of life is in the mundane. In the little moments. The morning hug, the first coffee, the sunrise. It's the chat with a friend you didn't expect to run into. It's the beautiful view out the window and the warm sun on your face. It's the home-cooked meal made with love, the goodnight text, and the early night snuggled in a warm bed. When you look back on your life it's these little moments that you'll be replaying in your memories and longing for more of. It's these little moments that are the real magic. The real magic is in the everyday.

WOMEN

Every day is an opportunity to cheer on the women around you. Every day you can choose community over competition. Because the truth is, everyone is out there doing their best. She too has a dream and a passion and a little self-doubt. You are not in competition with each other. When you celebrate her, encourage her and cheer her on, you raise her up. We are all more similar than we realise and when we can bring our dreams, our hopes, our support, and our passions together, amazing things will happen. So share more love with the women around you today show more love to yourself. Let's create a world where building others up is what we do, because it is both powerful and beautiful.

START

Don't wait for tomorrow, for Sunday, for next week or next year. Today is the right time to take that action. To take a small step towards your dream. Today you can love yourself a little more. You can say yes to that opportunity that scares you. Or you can say no if you know in your heart it's not for you. Today you can have that conversation, book into that course. Get started with your health, love or work dream. Whatever you desire, you are wildly deserving of. And today is the perfect day to get started.

TRUSTING

Here's to knowing you are worthy. Here's to knowing this is just the beginning. Here's to knowing so much more is to come for you. If you are not yet where you want to be, here's to knowing you are on the way. Here's to knowing that you are doing your best. Here's to being you, unapologetically you. Here's to sharing your voice, your passions, and desires. Here's to being more you and ending each day with a grateful heart. Here's to trusting. Here's to knowing you are wildly deserving.

ABOUT LISA

Lisa is a writer, dreamer, multi-passionate creator and mother to two young boys living in Auckland, New Zealand.

www.lisabuscomb.com
@words_by_wilde_road

Made in the USA
Coppell, TX
10 September 2023

21443058R00063